the story of...

THE BUILDING OF THE
GREAT PYRAMID

Author
Colin Hynson

Consultant
Dr Nicholas Saunders

Pharaoh Khufu *Born 2589 BC, he was the son of the great pyramid builder Pharaoh Sneferu and Hetepheres. He reigned for about 24 years, during which he built the Great Pyramid of Giza. After Khufu's death in 2566 BC, his son Menkaure built a smaller pyramid at Giza, eventually completing the last of the famous pyramids at Giza.*

Pharaoh Sneferu *Father of Pharaoh Khufu and ruler of Ancient Egypt for approximately 24 years. This pharaoh was responsible for the building of the first true pyramid: the Red (or Northern) Pyramid. Due to its stability it was the model for all the main pyramids at Giza. It also served as Sneferu's final resting place.*

Pharaoh Narmer *Is thought to have been a ruler of the First Dynasty (3050 - 2890 BC). Evidence of his existence has been found in various parts of Egypt, but it is not yet clear which part he played as a ruler. Theories suggest that he and the legendary Men are in fact the same person.*

Queen Meritetes *Daughter of Pharaoh Sneferu and wife of Pharaoh Khufu. One of the pyramids of Giza is thought to have been built for her as her final resting place. She lived through the reigns of the Pharaohs Sneferu, Khufu and Khafre.*

Queen Hetepheres *Wife of Pharaoh Sneferu and mother of Pharaoh Khufu. Hetepheres was the daughter of Egypt's first pyramid builder, Khufwy and his sister-wife Merityetes II. She was buried in Dahshur, but her tomb was raided shortly afterwards, and her remains have never been found.*

Copyright © ticktock Entertainment Ltd. 2006
First published in Great Britain in 2006 by ticktock Media Ltd.,
Unit 2, Orchard Business Centre, North Farm Road, Tunbridge Wells, Kent, TN2 3XF
ISBN 1 84696 003 7
Printed in China
A CIP catalogue record for this book is available from the British Library.

CONTENTS

THE COUNTRY OF EGYPT

The great civilization that we know as Ancient Egypt arose around farming communities that settled on the River Nile. They relied on the Nile flooding so make the soil fertile so that they could grow their crops. The farmers also needed stability. Before the creation of the Egypt of the pharaohs there was continual conflict between different parts of Egypt.

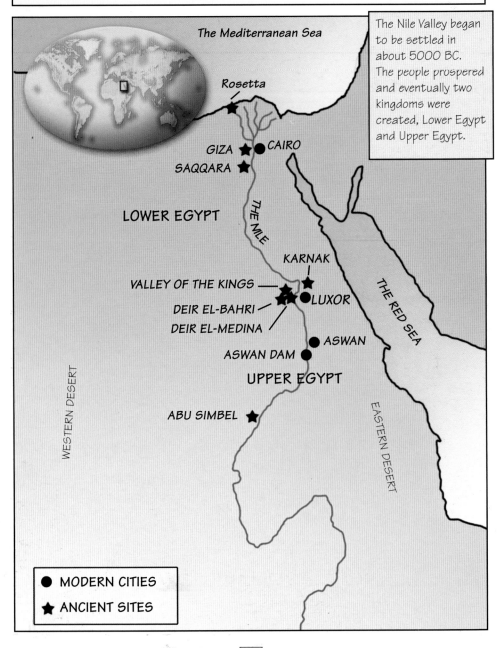

The Mediterranean Sea

The Nile Valley began to be settled in about 5000 BC. The people prospered and eventually two kingdoms were created, Lower Egypt and Upper Egypt.

Rosetta

GIZA ● CAIRO
SAQQARA

LOWER EGYPT

THE NILE

KARNAK

VALLEY OF THE KINGS

DEIR EL-BAHRI ● LUXOR

DEIR EL-MEDINA

● ASWAN

ASWAN DAM ●

UPPER EGYPT

THE RED SEA

WESTERN DESERT

ABU SIMBEL ★

EASTERN DESERT

● MODERN CITIES
★ ANCIENT SITES

In about 3000 BC the two kingdoms of ancient Egypt were unified by King Narmer. He conquered the north of the country and started the reign of the pharaohs.

Narmer made himself the first pharaoh of Egypt. Under his rule Egypt began to flourish. All of the pharaohs that followed him continued to make Egypt a powerful kingdom.

At last we can have some peace between the two kingdoms. Now we can get on with our farming.

Can you see who that is? It's king Narmer. I've heard that he is travelling through all the lands that he has conquered.

My lord, you now have control of all of this land. You must rule wisely.

I mean to do so. Tell all of the people that we now have peace, but that peace can only survive if they obey my orders.

FAST FACT The Nile flooded in August and September and then receded in October and November.

5

The first pyramid was built about 500 years after King Narmer brought the two kingdoms together. It was built by King Djoser as a tomb for him and his family.

Later my son, we have a lot of work to do first.

Father, can we go and see the tombs where our kings are buried? I've heard that they are so high you cannot climb to the top.

No! The fields are fertile and wet after the flood. We must use the time to plough the fields ready for our crops

Now can we go?

The annual flooding of the Nile covered farmland with silt, great for crops. When the water receeded, the land could be ploughed.

THE LIFE OF A PHARAOH

The pharaohs were not just the rulers of Ancient Egypt. They were also seen as living gods with a special link to the gods that they worpshipped. The daily life of a pharaoh followed a strict timeline.

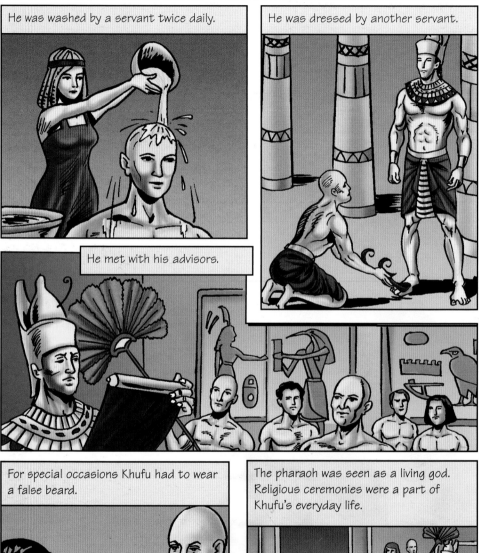

He was washed by a servant twice daily.

He was dressed by another servant.

He met with his advisors.

For special occasions Khufu had to wear a false beard.

The pharaoh was seen as a living god. Religious ceremonies were a part of Khufu's everyday life.

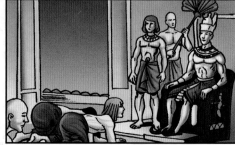

In about 2500 BC King Sneferu founded the 4th Dynasty of the kingdom created by Narmer. He was a powerful king who conquered lands all around Egypt. He also wanted to make sure that Egypt remained powerful after his death.

My lord, you must have a son. Then your power can be carried on for many years.

Father, can we go and see the tombs where our kings are buried? I've heard that they are so high you cannot climb to the top.

One day Sneferu's wife, Hetepheres, had some news for him.

I am expecting a child.

Good. Now my dynasty will remain safe.

A son. I have a son. We shall call him Khufu.

Because Khufu was such an important baby both Sneferu and Hetepheres wanted to make sure that their gods would bless him. They arranged for a special ceremony in a temple.

We call on the gods to look down on this boy Khufu. Make him grow and prosper and one day to rule this great land with wisdom and strength.

As Khufu grew he began to learn all of the things that he would need to know for when he became pharaoh. He was also allowed some time to play.

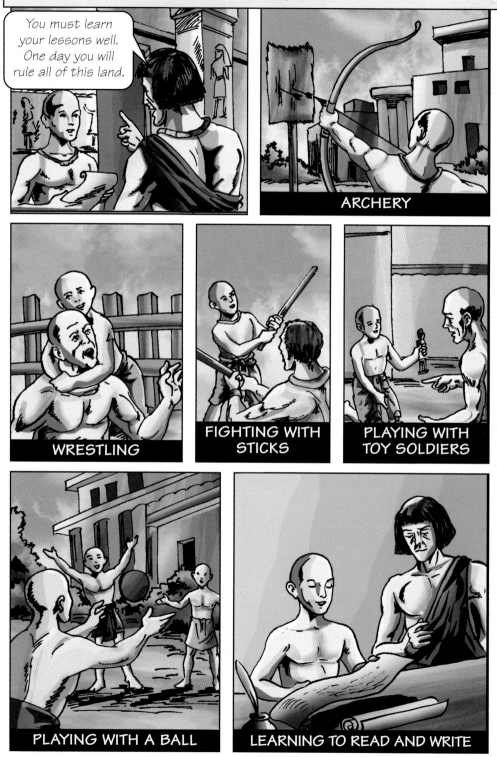

You must learn your lessons well. One day you will rule all of this land.

ARCHERY

WRESTLING

FIGHTING WITH STICKS

PLAYING WITH TOY SOLDIERS

PLAYING WITH A BALL

LEARNING TO READ AND WRITE

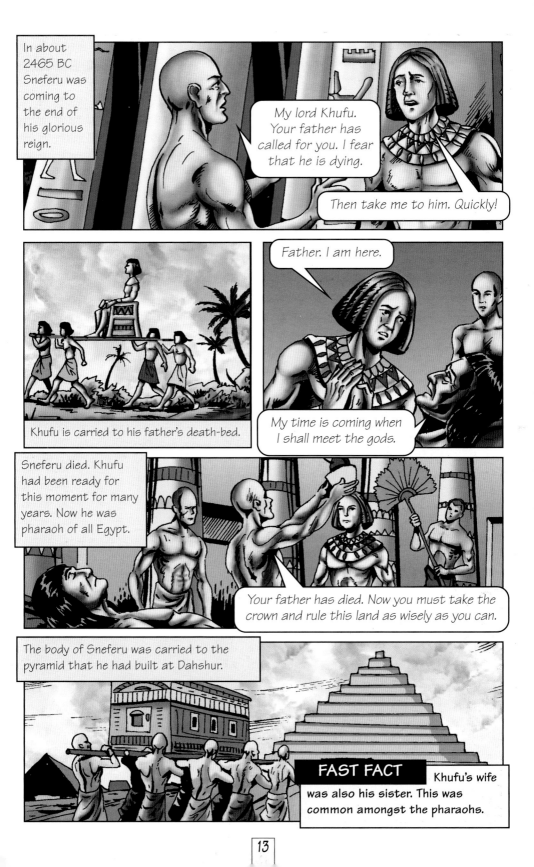

In about 2465 BC Sneferu was coming to the end of his glorious reign.

My lord Khufu. Your father has called for you. I fear that he is dying.

Then take me to him. Quickly!

Khufu is carried to his father's death-bed.

Father. I am here.

My time is coming when I shall meet the gods.

Sneferu died. Khufu had been ready for this moment for many years. Now he was pharaoh of all Egypt.

Your father has died. Now you must take the crown and rule this land as wisely as you can.

The body of Sneferu was carried to the pyramid that he had built at Dahshur.

FAST FACT Khufu's wife was also his sister. This was common amongst the pharaohs.

KHUFU'S BIG PLAN

One day Khufu decided to build a great pyramid to rival those built by his father. Building a pyramid required a lot of planning even before the first stones were laid. It needed not just lots of workers but also experts such as an architect and skilled stonemasons.

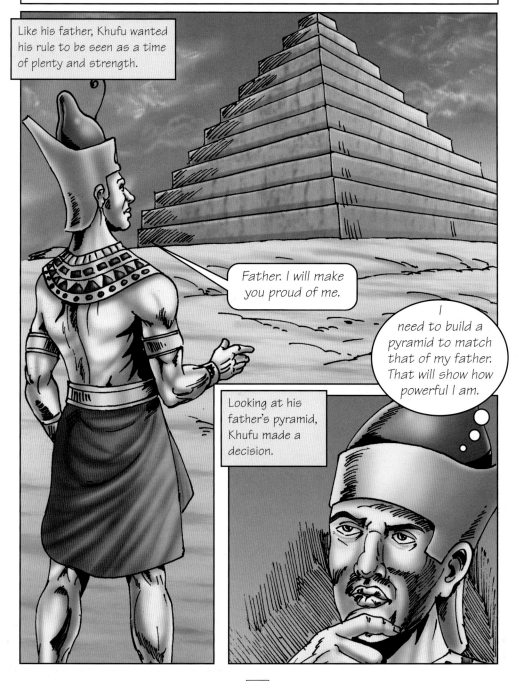

Like his father, Khufu wanted his rule to be seen as a time of plenty and strength.

Father. I will make you proud of me.

I need to build a pyramid to match that of my father. That will show how powerful I am.

Looking at his father's pyramid, Khufu made a decision.

Khufu met with his main advisor called a vizier. He told the vizier of his plans.

I agree with my lord. You must build a pyramid just as your father did. However, perhaps you should make your pyramid the greatest ever seen.

The vizier appointed an architect who drew up plans for the new pyramid.

My lord, you can see that this pyramid will not only be larger than your fathers but the sides will also be smooth. It will shine in the sun.

Very well. You must begin work soon. We will show the world that Egypt is more powerful than ever.

The farmers of Egypt gave part of their crops to the pharaoh each year. They were also expected to leave their homes and to work for the pharaoh for a few months each year.

We will need many thousands of labourers for the building of Khufu's pyramid.

I will put a list together. Each man in Egypt should be told to work on the building.

During the flood season, farmers had little to do but wait for the water level to drop. To make money during this time, many farmers went to work for the pharaoh.

The floods arrived. We will have a good crop next year.

Yes, but while the flood waters cover our fields we have little to do. I expect that we shall have to work for the pharaoh.

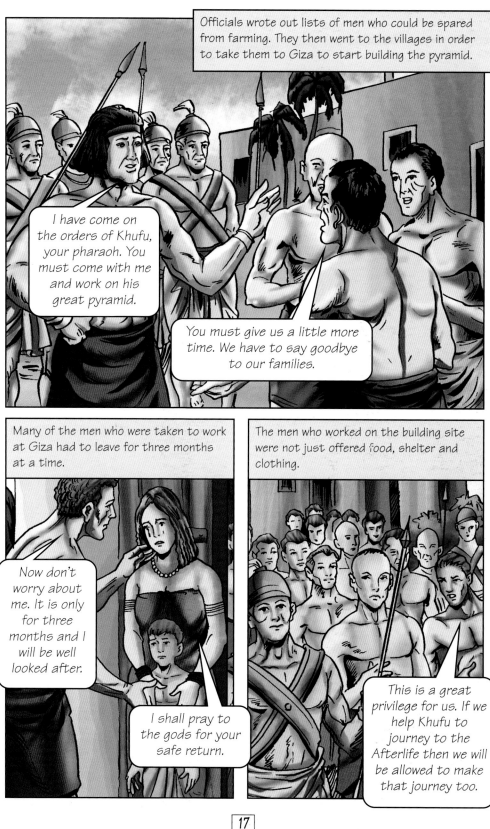

Before the labourers could be brought to start building the pyramid a site had to be chosen. It was decided that the pyramid was to be built on the west side of the Nile. This was for both practical and religious reasons.

This is a good site. It is never flooded by the river and it needs to be solid rock below the ground. It has to support a great building.

Yes, and this side of the river is dedicated to the god Osiris, the god of death and birth.

The pyramid had to built so that its four sides faced north, south, east and west. The ancient Egyptians did not have a compass so they relied on a priest to find north for them by looking up at the night sky.

Once this staff is between me and the Pole Star then draw a line on the ground between me and the staff.

Then we will know where north and south are.

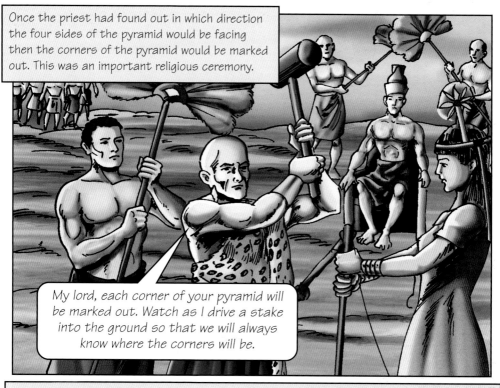

Once the priest had found out in which direction the four sides of the pyramid would be facing then the corners of the pyramid would be marked out. This was an important religious ceremony.

My lord, each corner of your pyramid will be marked out. Watch as I drive a stake into the ground so that we will always know where the corners will be.

Once these ceremonies were over then the building could begin. However, the first thing that had to be done was to level the land and lay the foundations for the massive structure to rest on.

How much more of these rocks do we have to carry away?

Pull! Everybody pull together!

I don't know but I'd rather be doing this than pulling those foundation stone. Now that's hard work.

FAST FACT About 4000 workmen worked on the pyramid all year around.

The stone used for the building the pyramid came from local quarries. The quarries had to be close to the river so that it could easily be carried to the building site at Giza.

This stone will be good for the inside of the pyramid.

Yes, it will. But we must go to Tura for the limestone and we also need granite. That will have to come from a great distance.

The quarry needed skilled stonemasons so that the blocks of stone could be cut accurately. It was important that they worked closely with the architect.

The blocks of stone were cut out of the rock and then shaped on the site. This had to be done without any kind of machinery.

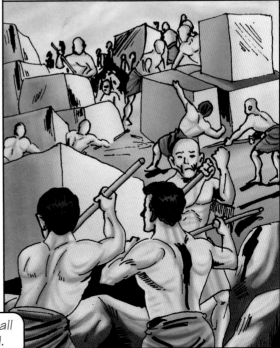

I will need all the labourers you can spare. We have many blocks of stone to carve out.

I will make sure that you have all of the workers that you need.

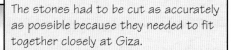
The stones had to be cut as accurately as possible because they needed to fit together closely at Giza.

You need to chisel a little more. This block needs to be a little smaller.

Wait a moment. Let me check that this side is smooth first.

When a block of stone was the right size and was smooth on all sides then it was ready to be taken to Giza.

You have to take time over that. If the block is not smooth enough then it can't be used.

At last we've finished. You took your time getting it smooth.

TRANSPORTING THE MATERIALS

Building a pyramid required a lot of planning even before the first stones were laid. It needed not just lots of workers but also experts such as an architect and skilled stonemasons.

Once the stones had been shaped and finished they had to be transported to Giza. The stones were taken by boat down the river Nile. However, the quarry was not right next to the river so the stones had be taken to the waiting boats.

Come on, put your backs into it.

Uurgh! I'll never complain about farming ever again.

Once the blocks of stone reached the river they had to be carefully lowered into the boat. The stones were so heavy that some of them slipped and fell onto the waiting boats.

The stone's falling. Watch out below.

Once the stones were on the boats they could then be rowed down the river to their destination at Giza. Boats full of stone headed towards the building site and empty boats went back to the quarry.

Slow down, this isn't a race. You'll have us over if you go too fast.

Once the stones arrived at Giza the stones were unloaded and then pulled up to the building site. The pyramid was growing in size.

The pharaoh said it was going to be bigger than his father's and he was right.

Look at the height of that.

FAST FACT Ancient Egyptian boats were made either from papyrus reeds or from cedar.

23

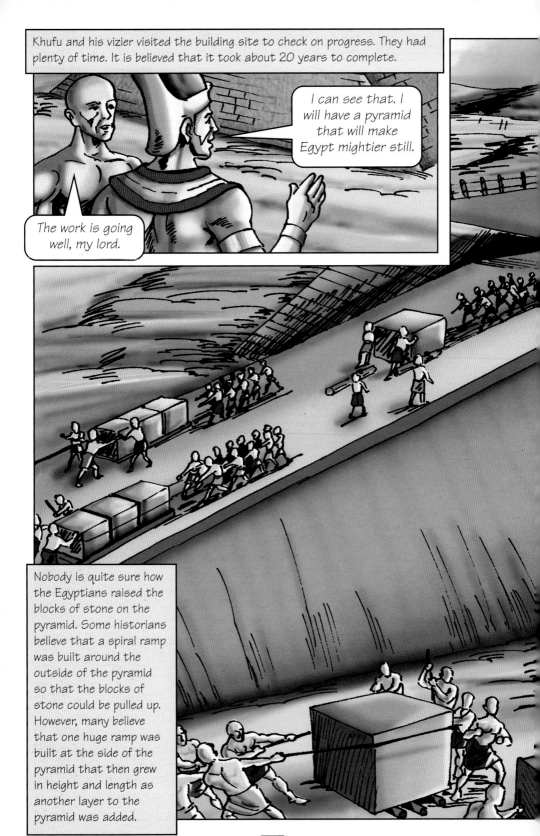

Khufu and his vizier visited the building site to check on progress. They had plenty of time. It is believed that it took about 20 years to complete.

I can see that. I will have a pyramid that will make Egypt mightier still.

The work is going well, my lord.

Nobody is quite sure how the Egyptians raised the blocks of stone on the pyramid. Some historians believe that a spiral ramp was built around the outside of the pyramid so that the blocks of stone could be pulled up. However, many believe that one huge ramp was built at the side of the pyramid that then grew in height and length as another layer to the pyramid was added.

Work on the pyramid took so long that children born when the pyramid was started were labourers a few years later.

Welcome son. Let me show you where you will be working.

Father. The pharaoh has called on me to build the pyramid. We'll be working together.

FAST FACT The ramp was made of compacted earth. A layer of mud on top made the stones easier to pull.

Whatever method was used it was hard work to pull the heavy stones up the ramp.

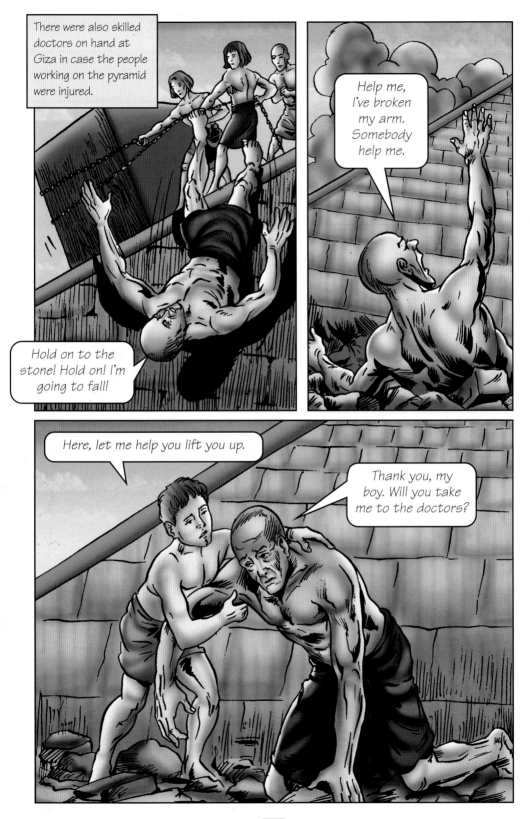

Doctor, my father has hurt his arm.

Bring him inside.

Ancient Egyptians doctors were skilled at looking after people. They used herbs as medicines and even knew how to mend broken bones.

I'm putting your arm in a splint. You will be out of work for a while.

Don't worry about me. My boy will look after me.

The broken bone mended and the splint was removed.

They're missing you at the Pyramid, father. They say they need your strength.

I'll be there soon enough, my boy.

Once the bone was fully healed then the labourer was back at work.

All together now. Pull!

FAST FACT Workers on the pyramid were divided into gangs. They had names like 'the Western Gang' and 'the Green Gang'

The labourers who built the pyramid were well looked after. They were given clothes, food and shelter. They worked about six hours a day with a rest in the middle of the day. There was time for them to relax and enjoy themselves.

Watch out for that snake. One bite and you're finished.

28

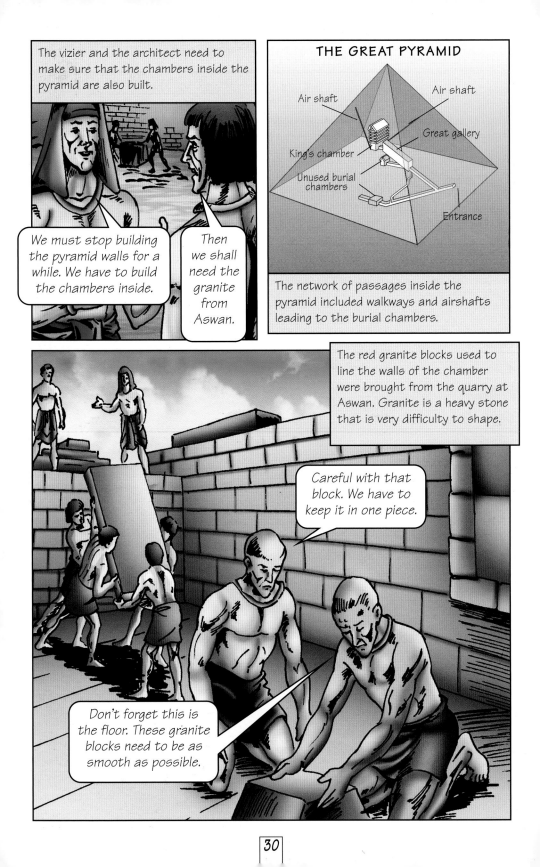

The vizier and the architect need to make sure that the chambers inside the pyramid are also built.

We must stop building the pyramid walls for a while. We have to build the chambers inside.

Then we shall need the granite from Aswan.

THE GREAT PYRAMID

Air shaft

Air shaft

Great gallery

King's chamber

Unused burial chambers

Entrance

The network of passages inside the pyramid included walkways and airshafts leading to the burial chambers.

The red granite blocks used to line the walls of the chamber were brought from the quarry at Aswan. Granite is a heavy stone that is very difficulty to shape.

Careful with that block. We have to keep it in one piece.

Don't forget this is the floor. These granite blocks need to be as smooth as possible.

The door to the main chamber in the pyramid was also made of granite. This had to pulled up into an upright position and then put in the right place.

I've got the block steady. Now ready and pull together!

Pull! Pull!

Sometimes mistakes were made and new ways had to be found to solve these problems.

My lord, the roof of the chamber will not be strong enough to bear the weight of the pyramid.

Then you will have to find a way to make it stronger.

To make the chamber roof strong enough we will have to put into five roofs on top of each other.

Five roofs? Five granite slabs. Do you know how heavy each of those blocks are?

The granite chambers are completed and the architect shows the vizier what has been built.

The pharaoh will be very pleased. This is a worthy tomb for him and his family.

FAST FACT The airshafts leading from the burial chambers point towards constellations of stars in the night sky.

Once the inside of the pyramid was complete then the white limestone blocks needed to be put on the outside.

The limestone blocks had to be lifted into place in the same way as all of the other blocks of stone. However, each of these stones had to be cut at the same angle and then carefully placed next to each other.

The walls of the chambers were painted and decorated. It was believed that these paintings had magical powers that could help the pharaoh in the Afterlife.

Mix that plaster well my boy. We have to make these walls smooth before they can be painted on.

Once the plaster was dry then a grid of red lines was painted on the wall.

Watch me carefully. Once we have a straight line then use the red paint.

An artist then drew the outlines also using red paint.

Corrections were then made in black paint.

The main colours to the painting were then added.

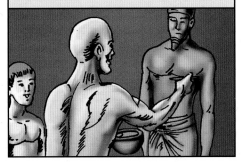

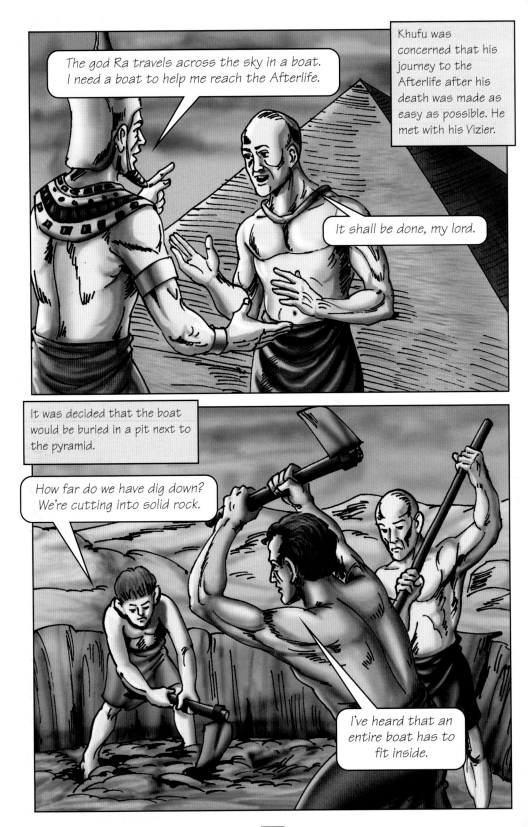

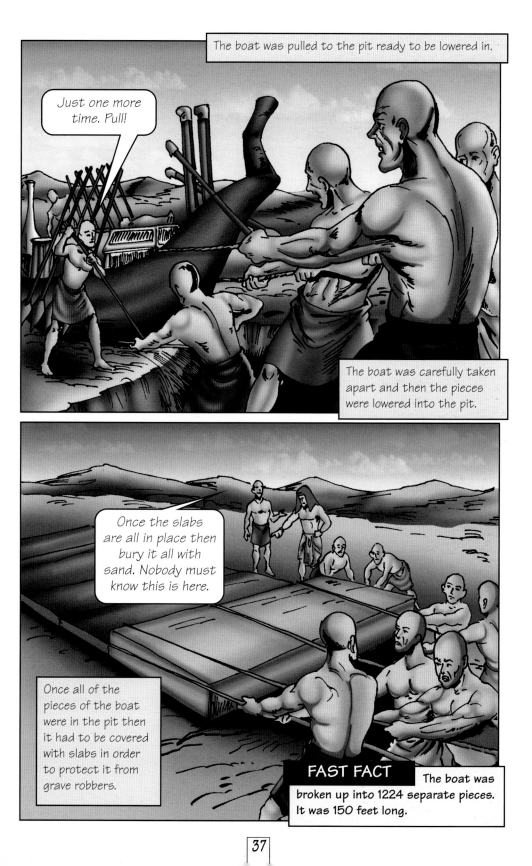

DEATH OF A PHARAOH

The Great Pyramid was built not just as a symbol of Egypt's power but also as a tomb for Khufu and his family. On his death in 2566 BC long preparations began for his body to be placed in the Great Chamber.

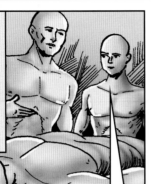

It was believed that if the body was allowed to rot then the soul could not travel to the Afterlife.

Surround his body with salt to draw out his fluids then fill with sawdust and linen.

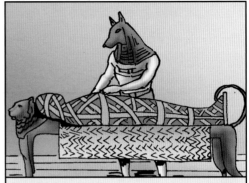

After Khufu's body was dried it was wrapped in linen bandages. This was done by an embalmer dressed as the god Anubis.

Khufu's body was then carried by boat to the temple that had been built near to the pyramid. The whole boat was then pulled up the causeway to another temple built next to the pyramid.

We need more oxen. We don't have enough to pull the boat all the way to the temple.

The most important ceremony was the 'Opening of the Mouth'. A priest used a special instrument to touch the eyes, ears, nose, limbs and mouth of the pharaoh.

As I touch you so you will see again, hear again, speak again, move again and speak again.

Be sure that the chamber is sealed first. Then we can escape by climbing along one of the tunnelss.

Once all of these ceremonies were finished Khufu was taken into the burial chamber inside the pyramid. He was placed inside a stone sarcophagus and everybody left the chamber.

FAST FACT Khufu's sarcophagus must have been put in when the chamber was built. It is too big to fit in the Grand Gallery.

No matter how well the pyramid had been built the treasures inside the chambers were too great a temptation for tomb robbers. By 1000 BC almost every pyramid in Egypt had been plundered.

In 641 AD Muslim invaders conquered Egypt. They were fascinated by these mysterious buildings.

The Muslim rulers found no treasure. However, in 969 AD they decided to build a new capital city at Cairo. They pulled off the limestone blocks to use as building material.

Carry on with your work. We will make our new city as glorious as these buildings once were.

The pyramids seen by modern tourists look nothing like the original pyramids. Only the top of Khufu's pyramid still has the original limestone casing.

Just take a picture. You know we're not allowed to take any of the stones from the pyramid.

This shows the whole complex of pyramids that were built by Khufu and by later pharaohs left today. The pyramid on the left was built by his son Khafre. The small pyramid is the Queen's pyramid. The buildings in front are the remains of houses for the labourers.

This picture shows all of the chambers and galleries inside the pyramid. It was once thought that there were three chambers because plans changed during construction.

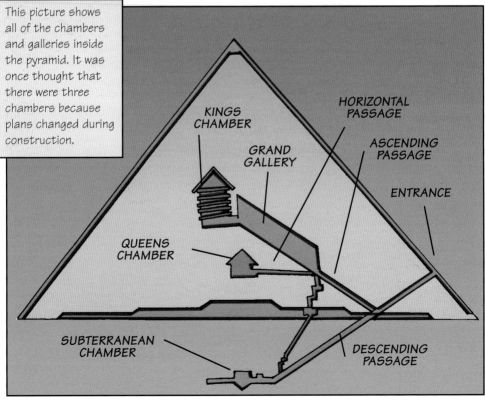

KINGS CHAMBER

HORIZONTAL PASSAGE

GRAND GALLERY

ASCENDING PASSAGE

ENTRANCE

QUEENS CHAMBER

SUBTERRANEAN CHAMBER

DESCENDING PASSAGE

This shows one of the passages that were built. They were very small and were meant to keep tomb robbers out.

This is the Queen's Chamber. It was too narrow for a body and was probably meant for a statue to lie in.

The Grand Gallery led to the King's Chamber. It was much bigger than all of the other galleries.

The King's Chamber measures 10 x 5 x 5 metres. Khufu was placed in a sarcophagus at the west end.

The civilisation of ancient Egypt was one of the largest and greatest the world has ever seen. Its ancient monuments, including its mighty pyramids still attract thousands of visitors every day. The great pyramid of Giza, built under the instructions of Pharaoh Khufu is the most famous of all. Egypt's ancient history after Khufu became very turbulent.

5000 BC: *The Nile Valley is first settled and farming begins*

3000 BC: *The two kingdoms of Upper and Lower Egypt were united by King Narmer.*

2700 BC: *The first pyramid was built by King Djoser. The Old Kingdom of Ancient Egypt is founded.*

2500 BC: *King Snefru founds the fourth dynasty of the Old Kingdom.*

2465 BC: *King Snefru dies and Khufu becomes the new pharaoh.*

2435 BC: *Khufu dies and is buried in the Great Pyramid.*

2100 BC: *The First Intermediate Period. For the next hundred years Egypt suffers from civil wars and famine.*

2000 BC: *Under the Middle Kingdom Egypt is reunited by a Prince of Thebes.*

1700 BC: *The Hyksos invade and conquer much of Egypt.*

1650-1550 BC: *The duration of the Second Intermediate Period.*

1550 BC: *The Hyksos are driven out and Egypt begins the New Kingdom.*

1504-1492 BC: *Reign of Pharaoh Tutmosis 1. He is the first Egyptian ruler to have a rock-cut tomb in the Valley of the Kings*

1336-1327 BC: *The famous Tutankhamun is made Pharaoh*

1279-1213 BC: *Under the reign of Ramesses II the temple at Abu Simbel is built*

1067-747 BC *The duration of the Third Intermediate Period*

747-332 BC *The duration of the Late Period*

525 –404 BC: *Egypt is invaded and become part of the Persian Empire. When the Persians are eventually defeated, the country returns to Egyptian rule*

450 BC: *The Greek traveller and historian Herodotus visits Egypt.*

332 BC - AD *395 The duration of the Greek-Roman period.*

343-332 BC: *Second invasion by Persia*

332-30 BC: *Egypt is conquered by Alexander the Great and the Persians are ousted from power.*

30 BC – 641 AD: *Egypt becomes part of the Roman and Byzantine Empires. Much of the country is converted to Christianity.*

641 AD: *Egypt is conquered by the Muslims.*

969 AD: *The limestone blocks of the Great Pyramid began to be removed to help build the city of Cairo.*

DID YOU KNOW?

1 *The Great Pyramid is 147 metres (482 feet) high.*

2 *The base of the Great Pyramid measures just over 230 metres.*

3 *The pyramids were believed to be staircases to heaven and were the preserve of the very rich and rulers.*

4 *The pyramids were a triangular shape so that one side always received the rays of the sun.*

5 *The Great Pyramid has 200 layers of stone from top to bottom.*

6 *There were very few slaves in Egypt and only a few of them were used in the building of the pyramids.*

7 *There are more than 80 pyramids in Egypt. Most of them are in ruins but a few survive. There are also surviving great temples, such as the one at Abu Simbel.*

8 *Cats were popular pets in Ancient Egypt. After they died they were often mummified and put into coffins.*

9 *It took about two weeks for Khufu's body was properly wrapped in bandages.*

10 *The average block of stone used on the Great Pyramid weighed about 2.5 tons. Some of the stones weighed over 15 tons.*

11 *When Khufu died professional mourners were hired who expressed the whole country's sorrow by singing to music.*

12 *Khufu's internal organs, like the heart or lungs, were mummified separately and placed in jars.*

13 *The Egyptians called the Afterlife the Field of Reeds. It was a place where the sun always shone and crops were always plentiful.*

14 *The paint used to decorate the Chambers in the pyramid were so expensive that they were locked away every night.*

15 *The tombs of the ancient Pharaohs were protected by curses. In order to make sure dead Pharaohs were safe inthe Afterlife, curses were made that stated that anyone who defiled a tomb would die as a consequence.*

16 *The discoverers of Tutankhamen's tomb, Lord Carnarvon and his team, were afflicted by a series of unfortunate events after their excavation of the tomb.*

17 *Lord Carnarvon himself died just five months after his great discovery from a mosquito bite.*

18 *Modern archaeologists do not believe in these curses. It is thought likely that spores growing inside the tombs and sarcophogi were responsible for the many deaths suffered by Egyptologists.*

GLOSSARY

Afterlife: *The belief that there is a new life after death. It was known in the Egyptians as the Next World.*

Anubis: *The guardian of the dead and the god of embalming.*

Architect: *Somebody who designs buildings. They also oversee the building being put up.*

Archeologists: *People who study history by digging up the past*

Capstone: *The pointed stone placed at the top of a pyramid*

Canopic Jars: *Jars that were used to hold mummified internal organs.*

Casing blocks: *Finely cut and polished blocks that form the outer layer of the pyramid*

Cataract: *A place where outcrops of rock interrupt the flow of the Nile. There are six in total.*

Causeway: *A raised path or road*

Cheops: *The ancient name for Pharaoh Khufu*

Citadel: *A fortress built on high ground above the city*

Civilisation: *A culture and its people*

Dynasty: *A family of rulers. Egypt had 31 dynasties.*

Egyptology: *The study of ancient Egypt*

Embalmer: *Somebody who preserves a dead body against decay.*

Fertile: *Land that is good for farming*

Hathor: *One of Egypt's oldest and most powerful goddesses, a mother who protects her worshippers in this world and the next. Her sacred animal was a cow*

Horus: *The god of the sky and of kingship. One of Egypt's most ancient gods, his sacred bird was the falcon*

Inundation: *A technical name for the annual flood that people depended on to grow food.*

Khnum: *God of the First Cataract, controller of the Nile. He fashioned people's bodies and spirits on the potter's wheel.*

Mortuary Temple: *The temple built against the side of a pyramid. The priests were supposed to make daily offerings to the dead king's spirit for all eternity*

GLOSSARY

Mummification: *The Egyptian method of preserving the body after death.*

Nubia: *Land to the south of Egypt, and an important trading country*

Opening the Mouth: *A ceremony that gives a dead person the power to speak, breath, feel and move again.*

Osiris: *God of the Dead, and ruler of the Underworld. He became part of Egypt's most popular deities.*

Papyrus: *Type of reed plant used to make many things, especially parchment to write on*

Pharoah: *This word comes from two words par-aa. It means 'great house'. It was a respectful way of referring to the King.*

Portcullis: *A gate or door that can be closed by sliding it downwards.*

Quarry: *A place where blocks of stone are cut out and shaped.*

Re: *The sun god, one of Egypt's most important deities. His main temple was at Heliopolis, north of Memphis.*

Sarcophagus: *A stone coffin. Only royalty and nobles could affore these expensive items. The body was placed in a wooden coffin and then put into a sacrophagus*

Sphinx: *A type of sun god. The one at Giza is the most famous, but there are other, smaller ones. It has a human head and the body of a lion.*

Stela: *An upright slab of stone or wood with inscriptions carved or written on it. The inscriptions are usually religious and record a special event.*

Thoth: *God of wisdom and medicine.*

Tomb: *A place where a dead person's body is buried*

Two Lands: *Term used to explain that Egypt started off as two separate kingdoms – Upper (southern) and Lwer (northern) Egypt.*

Valley temple: *A temple in a straight-sided pyramid complex. It stood where the valley met the desert*

Vizier: *One of the pharaoh's most important advisers and minister.*

Underworld: *Another realm inhabited by the dead. Every day the god Re had to sail through the Underworld to ensure the Sun rose in the morning.*

INDEX

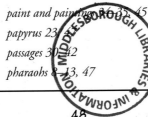